GOD GIVEN DREAMS

One Evidence God Communicates
With His people.

Irma Gottshalk | MT. Sinai Retreat | Jamaica

Verbal, Physical, Sexual Abuse Note:

If you are experiencing any form of abuse, I pray God gives you the boldness and inner strength to speak up and reach out to someone who can truly help you. You are worthy of protection, respect, and love. While I may have only touched on this briefly in my writing, let me be clear, abuse is never acceptable and must never be minimized.

A Mental Health Note:

If you have dreams that terrorize you, and or telling, causing you to hurt yourself, someone, or property, please seek a mental health provider.

"Beloved, I wish above all things that thou mayest prosper and be in health even as thy soul prospereth." - 3 John 1:2 (KJV)

Dedication

All glory and honor to God, the author and finisher of our faith. Hebrews 12:2 (KJV).

This book is dedicated to my beloved daughter, Xoana Marissa Gottshalk, the dreamer. She had dreams of the pain she was experiencing; and as her mother, I did not make the connection. I did not take her dreams seriously enough, even though I experienced dreams of my own.

In one of the chapters, I will share the dream I received about Xoana's death. When she mentioned she had a dream, I took it lightly, because one of the times, I was like, *"Are you Joseph?"*

The second dedication is to parents and children. Matthew 19:14: *"But Jesus said, Suffer (allow/permit) the little children, and forbid them not, to come unto me: for such is the kingdom of heaven."*

So many children around the world have experienced trauma, and I am one of them. As a mother who has experienced the death of a child, I have become a firm believer that every child should know who Jesus is.

The Bible warns us: *"Be alert and of a sober mind. Your enemy the devil prowls around like a roaring lion looking for someone to devour."* 1 Peter 5:8 (NIV).

If we as adults are vulnerable and naïve to the schemes of the enemy, our children are even more vulnerable.

This framed collage is Xoana's last science school project.

Acknowledgement

I ran to Kingdom Life Church. They prayed for me and my family through a difficult time in our life.

This picture was taken on 16 August 2025 with the Women of Royalty Pop-Up Prayer, Lion's Park, Killeen, Texas. I debated about getting a formal picture, but the representation of these prayer warriors walking and praying in faith in the open air is more powerful than being dressed up.

Lindia (Daughn) Gottshalk, *Trusted Proofreader*

Daliaan James, *Founder, Each One Lift One & Certified Christian Life Coach*

Kasba Degrate, *IMPAC Outreach*

Dr. Kerry-Ann Zamore-Bryd, *CEO, KZamore Enterprises LLC.*

Table Of Content

Foreword

Dr. Kerry-Ann Zamore Byrd

In the five years that I have known Chef Irma, she has been nothing short of a blessing to me, my family, and the many communities I serve. From the very beginning, she has demonstrated not only her extraordinary skill as a chef and caterer but also her heart, her vision, and her deep sense of purpose in all that she does.

What makes Chef Irma so remarkable is that her talent extends far beyond preparing meals. She has the unique gift of creating experiences. Every event she touches becomes more than a gathering; it becomes a memory, a moment of joy, and, most importantly, a fulfilled dream.

Over the years, Chef Irma has catered for some of the most important occasions in my life and the lives of those I hold dear. From intimate family birthdays to elegant wedding receptions, she has consistently exceeded every expectation. She has also poured her talents into larger community events, catering for my sorority, Jack and Jill of America, Incorporated, and The Links, Incorporated chapter functions.

And, without question, her eye for curating the most exquisite tea parties has become one of her signature gifts, each table a delicate masterpiece of color, flavor, and charm that leaves guests enchanted. At every level — whether personal or professional — Chef Irma brings the same unmatched level of excellence, thoughtfulness, and creativity.

One of the qualities I most admire about Chef Irma is her extraordinary attention to detail. She has a gifted eye for capturing the theme of any event and enhancing it with her own beautiful and distinctive touch. She carefully considers every element — the colors, the flavors, the textures, the presentation — and seamlessly weaves them together into a design that is not only delicious but breathtakingly beautiful. Her work reflects true artistry, one that demonstrates her respect for food as well as her respect for the people she serves.

Her knowledge of cuisine is both expansive and inclusive. With a deep understanding of flavors and traditions from around the world, Chef Irma brings a global awareness to her work that honors cultures while still tailoring each menu to the heart and story of the event. Whether it is a classic comfort dish or a sophisticated international entrée, she prepares each plate with precision, love, and a respect for its origin.

She doesn't just serve food — she tells a story through every dish, making sure that all who partake feel seen, valued, and celebrated.

Beyond her undeniable professional gifts, Chef Irma has become more than a chef and caterer in my life — she has become a friend. Her warmth, generosity, and integrity shine through in everything she does. Working with her is never simply about the food or the event; it is about partnership, trust, and shared joy.

She has the rare ability to truly listen, to understand the vision of her clients, and to transform that vision into reality in ways that surpass what anyone could have imagined. Time and again, she has proven herself to be not only reliable but also inspiring, making each collaboration a delight.

It is no exaggeration to say that Chef Irma makes dreams come true. She embodies the very spirit of this book's title, *God-Given Dreams*. Through her culinary gifts, her artistry, and her heart, she brings to life events that people only dared to imagine. She infuses every occasion with beauty, flavor, and love, leaving behind not just satisfied guests but cherished memories that last a lifetime.

As you turn the pages of this book, may you catch a glimpse of the incredible talent and passion that I and so many others have been privileged to experience firsthand. Chef Irma is more than a chef; she is a visionary, a storyteller, and a vessel of God's grace through food.

It is an honor to know her, to work alongside her, and to witness her dreams continuing to blossom.

With gratitude and admiration.

Preface

Purpose

The first purpose for writing this book is because God put it in my spirit. I procrastinated, but it still came back to me. Before I wrote the first cookbook, I had this book. I swear I was not going to write another book because of the ordeal that went on with the first cookbook, but the Holy Spirit reminded me that I had this one to write.

I wrote a second cookbook. I went to Africa and was inspired to write a third cookbook, and the Holy Spirit reminded me again that I had this book about dreams to write. I was not certain what or how to write, but once I settled down and started writing, the Holy Spirit started to download what to write.

The second purpose is: Why is God communicating with us? He communicates with us because He wants to build a relationship with us, get us to know who He is, guide us into His will and purpose, fill us with His love and covenants, lead us to repentance and salvation, and equip and encourage us.

Dreams are just one of the ways God communicates with His people. I intentionally use the word *communicate* versus *speak/talk* because if I use the word *speak/talk,* then someone may just be listening for an audible voice or a sound.

Here are some relational scriptures that back up who God says He is to us, and His expectation for us:

Exodus 20:2–3 states, "I am the Lord your God, who brought you out of Egypt, out of the land of slavery. You shall have no other gods before me."

John 10:27: "My sheep listen to my voice; I know them, and they follow me."

The scripture I stand on that shows God communicates with us through dreams comes from Job 33:14–17:

"For God does speak—now one way, now another—though man may not perceive it. In a dream, in a vision of the night, when deep sleep falls on men as they slumber in their beds, He may speak in their ears and terrify them with warnings."

"Though man may not perceive it" is the part that stands out to me, because I find myself guilty of not comprehending that these dreams are significant, and it's God communicating with me. There are various scriptures throughout the Bible where God speaks to His people in dreams.

God speaking to His people through dreams is not a new concept. Throughout this book, I will refresh your memory with some of those scriptures where God communicates with His people through dreams.

The Goal

The goal of this book applies to me first, the writer. Second, to the reader—that we should begin and stay in communication with God by listening and speaking with Him regularly, and by reading and meditating on His word.

Two scriptures that tell us the benefits of knowing God's word are:

Deuteronomy 17:19 (NIV): "It is to be with him, and he is to read it all the days of his life so that he may learn to revere the Lord his God and follow carefully all the words of this law and these decrees."

Joshua 1:8: "Keep this Book of the Law always on your lips; meditate on it day and night, so that you may be careful to do everything written in it. Then you will be prosperous and successful."

God communicating with us in dreams does not replace us praying and reading the word of God. This is just one way God communicates with His people. If we are getting dreams from God, let us please pay attention.

There are dreams that may come from our subconscious or from the enemy, but knowing the word of God will help us decipher if God is speaking to us.

Each chapter offers a dream or prayer journal, inviting you to reflect, grow, and put into practice lessons learned.

I hope you perceive it.

Chapter 1

In the Beginning

"And he shall be like a tree planted by the rivers of water, that bringeth forth his fruit in his season; his leaf also shall not wither; and whatsoever he doeth shall prosper".

— Psalm 1: 3 (KJV)

Dream Journal

Date: _____

Time you woke up: _____

Title of the Dream: _____

The Dream (Detailed Description):

_____

_____

Emotions Felt (Peaceful, Afraid, Confused, Joyful, Urgent, Other):

_____

_____

_____

Interpretation:

_____

_____

_____

Scripture or Insight:

_____

_____

_____

Manifestation (which may come later):

_____

_____

_____

My earliest memory of a dream was when I was a child, around the time I was in grade one. This was a recurring dream of a man under a tree, always watching me. The dream was bothersome to me, and I told my stepmother (Amanda Morrison) about it. She told me if I had the dream again, I was to confront the man.

The dream came again, and I somehow confronted him. I don't remember how, but I never saw him again. As I write this book, I decided to research the meaning of this dream. The interpretation was spot on: "The dream could be an expression of a subconscious need for safety or protection, possibly stemming from real-life anxieties or perceived threats."

I was three years old when my biological mother dropped me off at the airport where my father worked. Later in life, I learned she was also given away as a child to her aunt, who was unable to have children, and was then abused by the aunt and her husband.

My mother also gave three other children to their father. I experienced molestation, physical abuse, and emotional abuse from my father. However, by the grace of God, my father sent me to church and forced me to read the Bible. The fact that my father sent me to church does not excuse his actions. By God's grace, I can forgive, but forgiveness does not mean excusing what was wrong.

I remember repeatedly reading Psalm 1:1–6 (NKJV):

"Blessed is the man who walks not in the counsel of the ungodly, nor stands in the path of sinners, nor sits in the seat of the scornful; but his delight is in the law of the Lord, and in His law he meditates day and night.

He shall be like a tree planted by the rivers of water that brings forth its fruit in its season, whose leaf also shall not wither; and whatever he does shall prosper.

The ungodly are not so, but are like the chaff which the wind drives away. Therefore, the ungodly shall not stand in the judgment, nor sinners in the congregation of the righteous. For the Lord knows the way of the righteous, but the way of the ungodly shall perish."

As a child, I sometimes remembered being the only one in the house going to church. This is why I have become a strong believer that children ought to know who Jesus is.

In March 2025, my sister Keisha and I sat with Aunty Maud in Jamaica as she imparted wisdom to us. She stressed the importance of praying for and over our children. "Pray against generational curses," she said. "We don't know what type of life the generation before us lived."

In recent years, someone had shared with her the character and life of her grandmother, who she never met.

One of God's principles for parents, found in Proverbs 22:6 (KJV), states: "Train up a child in the way he should go; and when he is old, he will not depart from it." The godly lessons instilled early will stay with us, even when we go astray for a time. We've all experienced that consistent training usually produces lasting results.

I have laid out my foundational life experiences as a child, but despite these trials and tribulations, God is my Savior and Deliverer. God gets the glory.

In the next chapter, I will scientifically clear up my misconception about dreaming.

Chapter 2

Are dreams a figment of our imagination?

"Thy word is a lamp unto my feet, and a light unto my path".
— Psalm 119:105 (KJV)

Prayer Journal

A great praying method to practice is Adoration, Confession, Thanksgiving, Supplication (ACTS):

Date: _____

Scripture: *Matthew 6:9–13 (KJV) — "Thy kingdom come, Thy will be done in earth, as it is in heaven."*

Adoration (Praising and worshiping God for who He is):

_____

_____

Confession (Repenting one's sins and asking for forgiveness):

_____

_____

_____

Thanksgiving (Thanking God for all His blessings, answered prayers, protection, and daily provision):

_____

_____

_____

Supplication (Bringing our requests to God for ourselves and others):

_____

God, our Creator, communicates with His people even when we don't accept Him as Lord. We are encouraged in religious settings to pray and read the Word of God daily. But I know our God loves us and still communicates with us even when we fall short.

There are various scriptures in the Bible where God communicates with someone who, by all accounts, was far from righteous. One example is King Abimelek, a pagan king in *Genesis 20*. Abraham told a half-truth that Sarah was just his sister. God came to Abimelek in a dream, stating: *"You are as good as dead because of the woman you have taken; she is a married woman."* The king confronted Abraham and returned Sarah with gifts.

The bottom line is this: God is the Creator of our body, mind, soul, and spirit, and He has the capability to communicate with His creation through dreams and many other methods.

The chapter's topic question is: *"Are dreams a figment of our imagination?"*

At first, I thought "figments of our imagination" meant something we make up in our mind that means nothing — something insignificant. But through the manifestation of some significant dreams, I grew far away from that misconception.

I knew there was a scientific explanation for why we dream, but I couldn't articulate it. So, I used AI professional assistance to define *figment* and *imagination* as they relate to dreams, and then I put them together. In essence, yes, dreams are a figment of our imagination — but they are significant, especially when they are from God.

Figment is generally defined as something invented or imagined; something that has no physical reality. By that definition, a dream is a figment — because the people, places, and events in a dream don't physically exist in that moment. They're mental constructs, not external realities.

However, here's the nuance: while the content of a dream is a figment (the dream characters, scenes, or stories), the experience of dreaming is real. The brain activity, the emotions you feel, the memories being processed — those are physiological and psychological processes.

So, you could say:

- Dream characters and stories = figments of imagination
- Dreaming itself = real brain event

Put simply, dreams are figments that come from real processes in your mind.

Imagination, in general, is the mind's ability to form images, ideas, sensations, or concepts that are not directly perceived through the senses at that moment. It's how you can picture an apple when there's no apple in front of you, or invent a story, plan your future, or daydream about flying.

When it comes to dreaming, imagination is at work in a unique, automatic way:

- While dreaming (especially during Rapid Eye Movement [REM]* sleep), your brain spontaneously creates images, sounds, characters, places, and scenarios — without your conscious control.

- Your imagination draws on stored memories, emotions, fears, wishes, or even random neural activity, weaving them together into a vivid experience that can feel real.

- Unlike waking imagination, where you choose what to imagine, dreaming is more like your imagination running on autopilot — generating surreal stories and scenes that surprise you.

So, in short: in dreaming, imagination is the mind's ability to create an internal world while you sleep — blending memory, emotion, and invention into a temporary reality that feels real while you're in it.

In one sense, dreams are a product of our imagination: they're mental experiences created by the brain, usually while we sleep, without direct input from the outside world. Our brains take memories, thoughts, emotions, and sensory impressions and weave them together into often surreal narratives. So in that sense, dreams are imagined.

However, dreams are not just random "figments" — they're also real psychological and neurological events. They involve complex brain activity, memory processing, emotion regulation, and sometimes even problem-solving. Neuroscience shows that during REM sleep (when vivid dreaming is common), certain brain regions are highly active, especially those linked to imagery and emotion, while parts responsible for logical reasoning and self-awareness are quieter — which is why dreams can feel vivid yet strange.

So, in short: dreams are imaginative creations, but they are also a natural, meaningful part of how our brains work — not merely empty illusions.

In essence, dreaming is a real experience that takes place in our brain. Now that we've cleared that up, we can venture into the next question: *"When I dream, what do all the dreams mean, and how do I get the interpretation?"*

Rapid Eye Movement (REM) is a stage of sleep characterized by quick, darting movements of the eyes, vivid dreaming, and increased brain activity. It's the stage where your mind is most active while your body stays mostly still, thanks to temporary muscle paralysis that prevents you from physically acting out your dreams.

Chapter 3

How to Seek God for the Interpretation of Our Dreams

A man's heart plans his way, but the Lord directs his steps.
—Proverbs 16:9

Dream Journal

Date: _____

Time you woke up: _____

Title of the Dream: _____

The Dream (Detailed Description):

_____

_____

Emotions Felt (Peaceful, Afraid, Confused, Joyful, Urgent, Other):

_____

_____

_____

Interpretation:

_____

_____

Scripture or Insight:

_____

_____

Manifestation (which may come later):

_____

_____

You woke up from a dream and you remembered the details. You dismissed it as nothing — it's just heartburn; you ate too much before you went to bed. Or another thought pops in your mind: what does this all mean? You share the dream with your spouse, a loved one, and eventually God. What does this dream mean? The bottom line up front (BLUF). You can forget about going to Ms. Clara, the neighborhood psychic, or online psychics. In Genesis 41:16 Joseph states, "Interpretation belongs to God."

Our Creator is omnipresent—present everywhere at once; omnipotent with unlimited power; and omniscient- possessing complete knowledge of the past, present, and future. Beyond these attributes, there is also His manifest presence—the moments when you tangibly sense God drawing near. Don't be surprised when His presence meets you in praise and worship, in prayer, in reading His Word, and beyond. Considering God's attributes, we can confidently seek Him for clarity of our dreams, and for what action He wants us to take, and when.

After Xoana's passing, I decided to execute some paperwork for my half-siblings on my biological mother's side. In less than three months I had a dream where I was in a beautiful garden, and about two or three lizards started crawling on me close to my neck. They seemed friendly enough, but I hate lizards. There is more to this dream. I sensed the Holy Spirit nudging me to share this dream with these siblings. My oldest sister told me, "Dreams don't always walk straight," meaning dreams are full of imagery that represents other things and are not always straightforward. One of the siblings eventually shared they were having a child — new birth is one interpretation when you dream about lizards. Dreams have hidden messages that don't reveal themselves until later in life. They can also have several meanings, but which one is applicable to you? So, believe now: you must go to God. I had that dream in 2018, and it was not until March 2025 — while writing this portion of the book — that another character of the dream was revealed. The full character of some of the siblings I was dealing with was revealed. Dreams of lizards also represent an enemy.

Here are some Bible-proven recommendations on how to get the interpretation of your dreams. This is not some magic potion. These recommendations go beyond dream interpretation; they will strengthen and grow your relationship with God. God loves us unconditionally and His desired relationship for us is one of fellowship, trust, obedience, redemption, and eternal covenant.

1. **Praise and Worship**

   One way to receive or to hear from God is through praise and worship. Psalm 95:1–4: "O come, let us sing unto the Lord; let us make a joyful noise to the Rock of our salvation. Let us come before His presence with thanksgiving, and make a joyful noise unto Him with psalms. For the Lord is a great God, and a great King above all gods. In His hand are the deep places of the earth: the strength of the hills is His also." Just in case the first scripture did not convince you, Psalm 100:4 says, "Enter into His gates with thanksgiving, and into His courts with praise: be thankful unto Him and bless His name." Worshipping God includes praise and thanksgiving, prayer, obedience, sacrifice, singing and music, reflection, and reverence. Worship is both internal and external. I enjoy worshipping and praising God because it takes me right into His presence. Worship music gives me this assistance. There are so many different genres of praise and worship songs — for example, Darlene Zschech's "God Is Fighting For Us" and "I Thank God" (feat. Maverick City Music — Upperroom).

2. **Praying and Seeking the Lord for His Guidance**

   Praying to the Lord for guidance is speaking to Him in your natural tongue or your spiritual language, asking Him to reveal to you the meaning of the dream. Does the dream pertain to me or someone else? Is this affirmation, confirmation, provision, protection, or a warning? How do you continue to pray about the outcome or against the outcome?

   When we don't ask God first, or don't ask at all, we run the risk of missing a warning message. When you experience the outcome, you will be like, "Oh my God!" Or you may come to the realization that God is real, and He really communicates to His people through dreams.

Here are some biblical principles to exercise when praying:

a. Pray in the Spirit — There is a prerequisite in Ephesians 6:10–18 for us to put on the full armor of God; and the way to activate and sustain that is to "pray in the Spirit on all occasions with all kinds of prayers and requests. Be alert and always keep on praying for all the Lord's people." (Eph. 6:18)

b. Ask God for understanding — James 1:5: "If any of you lacks wisdom, you should ask God, who gives generously to all without finding fault, and it will be given to you."

c. Pray without ceasing — 1 Thessalonians 5:17 means living in ongoing awareness of God's presence, with a heart and mind stayed on Jesus.

d. Seeking God is part of praying, but deeper. It's the action of pursuing His presence, will, and truth with your whole heart. These actions are practical: saying thank you for His creation; asking for peace before a tough conversation; asking for wisdom before a tough decision; praising God while driving to work or going to school; praying for someone when they come to mind; and praying against anxiety instead of letting it fester.

3. Write Down the Dream

As soon as you wake up after a dream, write every detail you can remember — people, places, colors, emotions, and symbols. Sometimes the smallest detail carries meaning. I must work hard at writing down the dreams because I get excited and want to know what the dream means. I go running to my sister or my husband before asking God and writing down the dream. My sister Keisha is the one who told me to write down my dreams. I now have a journal on my nightstand.

4. Read Your Bible and Evaluate the Dream Through Scripture

We must read and study the Word of God for several reasons. One reason is we get to know God's character — this is how we build trust. 2 Timothy 2:15 states, "Study to shew thyself approved unto God, a workman that needeth not to be ashamed, rightly dividing the word of truth." If we don't know what is in the Bible, we won't know God's truth.

a. We must trust that God will not tell us to do anything that will contradict His Word. If the dream encourages something sinful or confusing, without peace, it's likely not from God. For God is not the author of confusion but of peace. (1 Cor. 14:33 NKJV)

In a dream, Granny motioned to me to remove my shoes. When I woke up, I immediately knew the dream was from God. Exodus 3:5 — "Take off your sandals, for the place where you are standing is holy ground." God's dreams warn, instruct, correct, give truth, clarity, conviction, protection, and peace. (See Genesis 37; Matthew 1–2; Daniel 2.)

b. Which brought me to this question: are all dreams from God? Specifically, evil dreams (dark, terrifying, deceptive, violent, tempting) are not from God. The enemy tries to sow fear, confusion, or temptation through dreams. In Job 4:13–17, Job's friend Eliphaz describes a dream he felt was from God; but in Job 42:7, God clarified that the dream did not represent His character. Our own mind or soul — stress, sin, trauma, or media — can influence our dreams (Ecclesiastes 5:3). False spirits or deception can masquerade as truth (2 Corinthians 11:14). This is when we must "plead the blood of Jesus" as soon as we awake. The Holy Spirit is here to assist us with this and in every aspect of our lives.

5. Seek Godly Counsel

Another option is to seek godly counsel from God-fearing and spiritually mature elders in your family or in your church for the interpretation of your dreams. God gives others the gift of interpretation (like Joseph or Daniel).

Please also pray about who to share your dream with for interpretation. In Genesis 40, the chief cupbearer and the baker went to Joseph while he was in prison to help with the interpretation of their dreams.

6. **VI. Look at the Symbols**

God often uses symbols that are familiar to us. What does this symbol mean in the Bible? What does it mean to me personally? How did it feel in the dream?

For example, a body of water may represent cleansing, the Holy Spirit, or emotional turmoil. Reference the symbols in Genesis 41 when Pharaoh dreamt about the seven fat cows that came up out of the Nile River, and then the seven thin ones that ate the fat ones—context matters.

7. **Consider the Context**

Dreams are not one-size-fits-all when it comes to interpretation; context gives us that clarity. A dream can be influenced by what's happening in our lives.

What emotions or decisions are we facing in the present? How do symbols appear in scripture or culture?

8. **It Is So Important to Wait for Confirmation**

"Wait on the Lord; be of good courage, and He shall strengthen thine heart: wait, I say, on the Lord!" (Psalm 27:14).

Don't act hastily or jump to conclusions. I acted hastily when I got a dream about me getting married. This was 27 years ago, and I am still embarrassed even as I type these words on this page. I entitled it, *"The Marriage Dream."*

Prior to 1998, in Arizona, I prayed earnestly and descriptively for a husband. I clearly heard in my spirit from the Holy Ghost: "No more description." I was so surprised—oh my God, God is real, He hears my prayers. I don't ever remember praying for a husband again.

Around 1998, while stationed in Massachusetts, I had a dream that I was going to get married to a pastor. In the dream, I was not shown the person. When I woke, and probably for several months, I allowed my imagination to run wild. I even did something that I won't share.

Two months later, saved by God's grace, I received a letter from Jamaica from my husband of now 26 years and counting. The gist of the letter: he asked if I was in a relationship, and if I was interested in having a relationship with him. I quickly responded, and we were married in 1999.

Kevin and I were friends in All Age School in Jamaica, and we would keep in touch every two years.

The lesson learned here is this: pray about your dreams. Don't jump to conclusions. If it's from God, He'll confirm it through scriptures, circumstances, or peace in your spirit.

You now have some biblical tools to understand your dreams, which come through praise and worship, praying, writing down the dreams, reading your Bible, seeking godly counsel, cross-referencing the symbols, considering the context, and waiting for confirmation. The God-given dreams do manifest.

Chapter 4

Living Through the Manifestation of a God-Given Dream

But after he had considered this, an angel of the Lord appeared to him in a dream and said, "Joseph son of David, do not be afraid to take Mary as your wife, because what is conceived in her is from the Holy Spirit."

—Matthew 1:20 (NIV)

Prayer Journal

A great praying method to practice is **Adoration, Confession, Thanksgiving, Supplication (ACTS):**

Date: _____

Scripture: *Mark 4:26–29 (KJV) — And He said, "The kingdom of God is as if a man should scatter seed on the ground, and should sleep by night and rise by day, and the seed should sprout and grow, he himself does not know how. For the earth yields crops by itself: first the blade, then the head, after that the full grain in the head. But when the grain ripens, immediately he puts in the sickle, because the harvest has come."*

Adoration (Praising and worshiping God for who He is):

_____

_____

_____

Confession (Repenting one's sins and asking for forgiveness):

_____

_____

Thanksgiving (Thanking God for all His blessings, answered prayers, protection, and daily provision):

_____

_____

_____

Supplication (Bringing our requests to God for ourselves and others):

_____

_____

_____

You got the dream. You applied the biblical tools for the interpretation. What do I do before the manifestation of the dream? The manifestation of the dream is the outcome of the dream; the dream has come to pass, which can be scary or exciting. Let's talk about how we handle the scary first.

"Plead the blood of Jesus." If this is something that is contrary to God's Word, find it in Scripture, and use Scripture to pray against it. I had a dream that some people were trying to get into my house or had gotten into my house — I don't quite remember all the details — but I did not get the sense in the dream that they were breaking in to steal my worldly possessions. I was able to call on the name of Jesus in the dream. When I woke, I grabbed my anointed oil, anointed the inside and outside of my front door, went to every door and anointed it, and anointed my children while praying everybody's favorite scripture: "*No weapon formed against me shall prosper, and every tongue that rises against me in judgment I shall condemn.*" (Isaiah 54:17). You pray to God that whatever that was will not come to pass, that it will bypass you and all your generations, and return to the pit of hell.

There are some occurrences in life that are out of our control, and learning to trust God with every aspect of our life is a process. So, the scary thing has manifested. The death of my daughter is the scary thing that manifested, which is addressed in more detail in Chapter 5. You are going to need some of those proven recommendations that I wrote about in the interpretation chapter such as praise, worship, and prayer. As I was driving and reflecting on a specific dream, I was reminded of the word "orchestrated." When Xoana passed away, I had an overwhelming feeling that our lives were orchestrated, because I dreamt about her death. Two scriptures came to mind: "Many are the plans in a person's heart, but it is the Lord's purpose that prevails." (Proverbs 19:21); and "The steps of a good man are ordered by the Lord, and he delighteth in his way." (Psalm 37:23). I needed a strong dosage of Philippians 4:7 to endure this difficult manifestation: "And the peace of God, which passeth all understanding, shall keep your hearts and minds through Christ Jesus." This is some supernatural, divine peace that goes beyond human logic.

Glory, hallelujah! I am ready for the goodness of God — the blessing, the healing, the deliverance, the good measure, pressed down, shaken together, and running over kind of manifestations. Aren't you? The front and back cover of this book represent the manifestation of a God-given dream.

Purpose and Provision

This dream has three parts. The first part is in Chapter 5; this dream is the second part; and the third part is not included in the book because I am unable to articulate it in its totality. The dream begins: I was with my sister Keisha, and we were on our family's property. At first, I was only aware of myself going through the rooms, and I realized that the house was completed. It was full of a bunch of things, but I told myself all I had to do was organize them. We then received a letter from a magazine company telling us that they were coming to do an interview about the property. One of us asked, "Why did you have the magazine company come out so soon? We weren't ready yet." My pastor appears in the dream and said, "Don't turn them away — let them come." Then Keisha and I said let's go see the rest of the land and what needs to be done, and we started to plant some stuff.

As Keisha and I were assessing the land, we realized the land was already planted and we did not have much more work to do. As we continued to assess the land, two boys showed up and my stepmother, Amanda, came into the dream. The boys were running around playing near a body of water that was spurting out water in the air. My mother stated that if they fell in, they were going to drop deep down in it.

When I woke up from that dream, I was so overjoyed, overwhelmed, unbelievably excited — I wanted to tell everyone. Words cannot express the joy I felt. Oh my God! Thank you, Jesus. I told my sister; I think I told my husband, my coworker friend Celia, maybe Aletheia, and my mother-in-law.

The Manifestation — Mt. Sinai Retreat (the house in the dream)

The house represents the physical manifestation of the dream given to me by God. Before my family and I migrated to the United States, we lived on our family's five acres of land in a semi-completed house; the living room was the only completed room. I felt like before Xoana's passing, my sister and I talked about this land and doing something with it. So after this dream, I believed and was convinced that the Lord was showing me to rebuild the house and do something with the land. Around the end of 2018, my sister, my brother Larry, and I had some serious discussions about the pros and cons of doing this project. The cons appeared to have won, because I sat on it for two years, exploring different ideas until COVID hit and I started watching YouTube where people were promoting Africa and returning to their homeland to build and establish themselves. I revisited the idea with my siblings again, and my brother gave me positive feedback. My father and I have an estranged relationship. I called him up and asked him if I could build a house on the land. He said yes — do what you want with it. I called my cousin Dermoth and asked him about this project, and he said he could handle it. I'd seen his work in the past, so I knew he was more than capable, and his mother Aunty Maud and her children are trustworthy. I began the house-building process, and God opened a door where I received a higher-paying job. I did not go looking for this job; this job came to me. I rejected it at first, and the Holy Spirit said to pray about it. I did and hurriedly made the call. God knew I was going to need some serious cash, because I thought building a 4,000-square-foot house in Jamaica was going to be dirt cheap, but it is not cheap.

Confirmation — The Road

In getting started, the biggest question was: should we fix the road first? This was also a question many years ago when my father was building on the land. It was partially fixed with sharp rock stones. This land had been neglected and overgrown with bushes for over 30 years.

Then a dream came to me: I saw my Granny, Florence Rowe — my stepmother's mother. She was coming up toward what I thought was Uncle T's house, and she was looking for someone. I told her the only person here was Tit (who is Uncle T's wife). Granny entered this wooden kitchen and motioned for me to take off my slippers. I don't remember if I took them off, but I was in the kitchen sitting beside her. After I woke up, the Scripture came to me: "God said, 'Take off your sandals, for the place where you are standing is holy ground.'" (Exodus 3:5). I asked her if I should build the road first. She did not give me an audible answer. The dream switched and I saw Granny in a beautiful embroidered tunic, and she was dancing. The tunic reminded me of the description of an ephod in the Bible. Exodus 28 gives an extensive description and purpose. In the dream I thought to myself that I didn't know Granny could dance. This was confirmation to me that I was on the right road and Granny was happy; but the Almighty God is the orchestrator. Outside the dream, Dermoth had to repair the road first because the trucks transporting construction materials would have a hard time climbing that rough, rugged road. In this dream, I was able to confirm through symbols, context, and Scriptures that this dream was from God — confirming I was on the right road.

Part two of the dream speaks of a material manifestation that is highly symbolic of the spiritual manifestation in part one of the dream. The Scripture I received comes from John 14:2 (KJV): "In my Father's house are many mansions: if it were not so, I would have told you. I go to prepare a place for you."

Dreams rooted in divine revelation carry the potential to impact lives and destinies. All dreams have the potential of manifesting, but we pray to God that those scary dreams don't manifest. Please praise God in all circumstances. (1 Thessalonians 5:18) "Give thanks in all circumstances; for this is God's will for you in Christ Jesus." In our next chapter, I share my God-given dreams of affirmation, confirmation, purpose, provision, and warning.

Chapter 5

God's Life-Alerting Dreams Provide Affirmation, Confirmation, Purpose, Provision, Protection, and Warning

Do not be anxious about anything, but in every situation, by prayer and petition, with thanksgiving, present your requests to God. And the peace of God, which transcends all understanding, will guard your hearts and your minds in Christ Jesus.
— Philippians 4:6–7 (NIV)

Dream Journal

Date: _____

Time You Woke Up: _____

Title of the Dream: _____

The Dream (Detailed Description):

_____

_____

_____

Emotions Felt (Peaceful, Afraid, Confused, Joyful, Urgent, Other):

_____

_____

_____

Interpretation:

_____

_____

_____

Scripture or Insight:

_____

_____

Manifestation (which may come later):

_____

_____

_____

When I was stationed in Arizona, I truly accepted Jesus Christ as my Lord and Savior — for real this time. I made a conscious decision: as for me and my house, I will serve the Lord until I die. It was time for discipleship. I became very conscious of the dreams again. Before this decision, I won't say I stopped dreaming, but if I did, I don't remember them.

In this chapter, I will share a few of my dreams of how God's life-alerting dreams provide affirmation, confirmation, purpose, provision, protection, and warning. God is not limited to these six subtitles — for you it may be different. Here begin some of the most life-changing dreams, which are organized by occurrence rather than by subtitle. The message in the dream may represent more than one subtitle.

Provision — Promotion

The first of these: I dreamt I was getting promoted to Sergeant/E-5. In the dream, I saw the actions that led up to me picking up the promotion packet. When I woke up, it was so real, overwhelming, and unbelievable all at the same time. In real life, I was the mail clerk for the Finance unit. I had to pick up the mail from the unit orderly room — the building I lived in — before I went into the office. The dream stayed in the back of my mind.

On April 1, 1996, I physically picked up my promotion packet and did not realize it until I started to distribute the mail. I called my brother and told him what happened. I was crying, and he said to me, "Why are you crying?" I said it was so unbelievable — I dreamt it, and it came through. I proceeded to tell him the dream.

Confirmation — Birth of our first child

When Kevin and I spoke about how many children we wanted, he already had a girl's name: Aletheia, which is the Greek word for truth. He learned the name in Greek class while at Bible college in Mandeville, Jamaica.

In 2001, I had a dream that someone was trying to steal my baby's name. When I woke up I told my husband about the dream. A few days later I realized I hadn't seen my period, so I asked my husband, "Did you see my period?" He was clueless too. I took an over-the-counter pregnancy test and sure enough — we were pregnant with Aletheia.

Warning — Our second child, Xoana

Xoana came on the scene on July 23, 2008. She had spunk; she was a warrior. She learned a scripture in Sunday school when she was about two or three years old that she loved to recite: Psalm 91:10–12 (NIV) — "No evil shall befall you." The rest of the passage reads, "No disaster will come near your tent. For he will command his angels concerning you to guard you in all your ways; they will lift you up in their hands, so that you will not strike your foot against a stone." There are so many lessons to be learned about God.

Xoana's declining health

Xoana's declining health was not apparent to us at first. Between 2017 and 2018, the signs in dreams started showing up for me. Xoana was already having some troubling dreams that I did not take seriously or did not know how to handle. She would not share the details when I asked her about them.

In second grade she started falling asleep in class, and some minor discipline issues started popping up — but at the time they seemed big. She was a talker who had no filters. We took her to the doctor's office, and she was eventually diagnosed with narcolepsy. This at first was believable to us because my father has narcolepsy, and Kevin had a relative with this illness as well. She was prescribed medication, but as time passed we felt like she didn't have narcolepsy and the medicine wasn't working.

At that time I owned a restaurant, and my lease was set to expire in September 2017. I struggled with the decision to close or renew. I told everyone I was wrestling with that decision. Eventually the Lord put it in my spirit that whatever decision I made would be okay. I closed the restaurant and went home to take care of my child.

After Xoana's death, I was so glad I had made the conscious decision to close the restaurant, because that choice helped me through the grieving process. When guilt tried to take over my mind, I reminded myself of what I had done to take care of my child.

We were in Houston one weekend when Xoana woke with a blood-curdling scream from a dream; she immediately called her grandmother to pray for her. Kevin and I got up and prayed for her, but she still would not share the dream.

Our family went to see the movie War Room. It was very moving, so shortly after that I cleaned out part of my closet to make a prayer closet. Xoana watched me and wanted me to start praying with her every night. I said the "Our Father" with her most nights, and then I realized she had memorized it. I wanted her to start doing it on her own, but she didn't let me off the hook. She would call out from her room for me to come and pray with her, and when I didn't go quickly she would holler again: "Mommy! Are you coming?" I would have to go.

Then I started to teach her Psalm 23 — "The Lord is my shepherd" — and she was catching on. Lesson learned for real: train your child in the way she should go, and when she is old she won't depart from it. Teach your children about God. God is real.

Warning that led to protection

I would say this was a warning dream that led me to run for protection. One night I dreamt someone came into my room and was literally suffocating me with a pillow. I had to plead the blood of Jesus. I got up that morning and told my two children we were going to Kingdom Life Church because of this dream. Xoana said to me, "I have worse dreams than that," but she would not tell me. I was not a member of that church yet, but I knew they were Holy Ghost-filled: they water-baptize, anoint you with oil, and pray for you. We went to the altar and the pastor anointed us and prayed over us.

Summer 2018 — my sister and I, with our two children, were planning to spend our summer vacation in Jamaica. Here comes another dream.

I dreamt we were at the beach and it was time for us to leave. Aletheia was by my side, but Xoana was playing in the sand and she showed up as a younger child. I motioned for her to come on, but she wouldn't — she was just sitting there smiling back at me. Keisha said, "I'll go get her," and as soon as she was about to step off to go toward Xoana, a train came by and got them, and the dream went dark. I thought the dream was about my sister because of a previous medical condition. I was worried we weren't going to make it to Jamaica. I told Keisha that morning about the dream and left it alone. My spirit knew something was up, but my mind could not grasp it. I couldn't put my finger on it, but something was wrong.

One day, I noticed two to three little blood bubbles that showed up on the inside of Xoana's mouth. I thought she was biting down on the side of her mouth. I had her brush her teeth and use Listerine. It seemed like they went away, but they came back up, and one morning she had blood all over the pillow.

We took her to the dentist the next day. He said it was her wisdom teeth coming in. My spirit knew something was wrong, but I couldn't put my finger on it. I wasn't satisfied with the dentist's answer, so I had Kevin take her to the doctor.

The doctor stated it was a virus going around and prescribed that pink antibiotic. I think the next week, she wasn't feeling well at school, and I took her back to the doctor. This became a big ordeal; we were under suspicion for abusing Xoana because she had welts on her arm. The doctor at the clinic didn't find anything medically wrong with her.

That night, she complained about her head hurting. I gave her Tylenol and sent her to bed. Early the next morning, I went to check on her, and she was not in her bed. I started screaming her name. She was on the floor at the foot of her bed.

We called 911. They tried to resuscitate her. I'm not certain if they did, but they took her to Seton Hospital. At the hospital, we were questioned, and I am paraphrasing the doctor's question and statement: "Is there anyone in the family who has a history of aneurysm? She was born with it, and she was going to die anyways."

They asked us about the marks on her arm. She took a ride on a helicopter to McLane Children's Hospital, where she went home to be with the Lord. I was told she was a fighter. Upon hearing the news, my brother Larry and my sister Keisha got on their way to be with us. Keisha reminded me of the dream, and I was like, oh my God—I had forgotten about the dream.

Child Protective Services (CPS) came to our home to investigate us because of the marks on her arm. A police detective was assigned to our case. We were in the process of finding a lawyer.

The next day, we were meeting the Pastor to plan the funeral. I think before we met with the Pastor, the detective came by and told us that Xoana died of cancer. Glory be to God; thank you for this relief. CPS closed the case in 30 days.

We got the autopsy several months later. Her diagnosis was Myeloid Sarcoma. The marks on her arms were superficial. They were a result of the cancer. Glory be to God, Hallelujah!

"I will bless the Lord at all times; His praise shall continually be in my mouth." Psalm 34:1 (KJV)

"God is our refuge and strength, a very present help in trouble." Psalm 46:1 (KJV)

"I will say of the Lord, He is my refuge and fortress: My God; in Him will I trust." Psalm 91:2 (KJV)

He is not only my provider, but also my deliverer.

Purpose & Affirmation – The dreams that came after Xoana's death

The last year of owning the restaurant, Xoana came up with us doing mother–daughter breakfast on Sundays. We went to two restaurants that served breakfast, but we favored one over the other.

Maybe less than a month after her passing, I went to the favored restaurant with my Bible. I sat and read my Bible in remembrance of her and had breakfast. I want to say the same night, 24 August 2018, I had a three-part dream. Part two is in the Manifestation chapter—this is part one of the dream:

In the dream, I came to a crossroad. I looked to my upper left, where there was a road leading to Mexico, and I said, I'm not going up there. But then I saw a man coming down with some kind of black aircraft outfit. In front of me was a helipad, and the man entered some type of black aircraft. I was scared to go that way also.

Then I looked to my right, and I saw a road leading to Canada, and thought, I can take that route. But in the dream, I did not actually take that route. I found myself in an aircraft. While on this aircraft, I saw a majestic glass building coming up out of the earth, and the aircraft was going around the outskirts of this gigantic hotel.

I was like WOW! This is a nice hotel. I've got to get the name of this hotel, because I'm going to this hotel. *Side note – When I woke up, I could not remember the name of the hotel to save my life.*

Anyway, I found myself in this brilliant and spectacular room with a gorgeous formal table setting. Someone said to me, "We are waiting for someone." I looked around the room with amazement, and eventually I saw Xoana sitting in this large aquarium with food in front of her. She did not have a happy look on her face.

I called out her name loudly, "Xoana, Xoana, Xoana!" Whoever this person was said, "She can't hear you." And I was out of that part of the dream and entered the second part of the dream.

Affirmation – Xoana is happy and in a better place

I had forgotten that I had prayed and written in my prayer journal that Xoana would be happy and in a better place. It was when I started to write this book and I started going through my prayer journal, I realized my prayers had been answered.

In this dream, I was sitting on a bench outside when Xoana came up to me excited and said, "Take a picture of me." I was so surprised—she caught me off guard. She started to dance her butt off and do flips, and I'm scrambling for the camera while trying to watch her dance at the same time.

I looked at her and said, "Xoana, I didn't know you could dance like that." I woke up out of the dream before I found the camera to take the picture.

In the next dream, we were at an outdoor game sitting on the bleachers. Aletheia and I were sitting below Kevin (their father) and Xoana. I motioned for Xoana to come down and sit with me and Aletheia, but she wouldn't come down. There was some type of commotion, and we found ourselves under a tree.

When I woke up, I clearly got the interpretation: Xoana was with The Father in heaven.

Another dream, I felt like I was summoned to go to the post office. I hadn't been to the post office in a while and had no reason to go there. So, I was in line, and I was excited that one of my favorite preachers was handing out letters to people in the line in front of me.

When it was my turn, he didn't hand me anything. Someone said he wasn't there to serve me. I was handed a letter, and it was a letter from Xoana. I opened it and saw that popular colorful Valentine's Day candy with the "XOXO," and a long letter.

I was still caught up about the preacher that I was unable to focus on reading the letter. I'm still kicking myself, because I was distracted and did not get a chance to read the letter.

In my defense—or guilt—I later read research that states we are unable to read in our dreams. Xoana was big on writing letters to express her feelings. I believe this was God's way of letting me know Xoana loves me.

What a lovely reassurance that God cares for us by providing purpose, warning, protection, provision, affirmation, and confirmation by communicating with us through dreams.

Chapter 6

Dreams Then and Now: A Timeless Human Experience

Then Jesus came to them and said, "All authority in heaven and on earth has been given to me. Therefore, go and make disciples of all nations, baptizing them in the name of the Father and of the Son and of the Holy Spirit, and teaching them to obey everything I have commanded you. And surely, I am with you always, to the very end of the age."

– Matthew 28:18–20 (NIV)

Prayer Journal

A great praying method to practice is Adoration, Confession, Thanksgiving, Supplication (ACTS):

Date: _____

Scripture: *Romans 4:21* – "And being fully persuaded that, what he had promised he was able also to perform."

Adoration (Praising and worshiping God for who He is):

_____

_____

Confession (Repenting one's sins and asking for forgiveness):

_____

_____

Thanksgiving (Thanking God for all His blessings, answered prayers, protection, and daily provision):

_____

_____

Supplication (Bringing our request to God for ourselves and others):

_____

_____

_____

The goal for this chapter is to show dreams from the Old to New Testament into the 21st century—from the Bible, which represents *then*, and two people who represent *now*.

This book continues to demonstrate the evidence that God communicates with His people through dreams, which is a timeless human experience.

I am a living witness, and I invited two friends in our community to share their God-given dreams.

According to *Joel 2:28*, "And afterward, I will pour out my Spirit on all people. Your sons and daughters will prophesy, your old men will dream dreams, your young men will see visions."

In *Daniel 2*, I am tickled by the story of King Nebuchadnezzar—because of the audacity—and amazed by the demonstration of God's supreme power and authority through Daniel.

The paraphrased story goes like this: The King had a dream that troubled his spirit. He called for his sorcerers, magicians, et cetera. He commanded them to tell him the contents of the dream (audacity!) and the interpretation by a certain time; if not, *death to you and your household.*

If they revealed the dream and its interpretation, then they would receive gifts and honor.

They said, "Oh mighty King, no man can do that—only the gods."

They searched for Daniel because he was included in the death decree. Daniel went to his three friends and asked them to pray for God's mercy.

God revealed the dream and the interpretation to Daniel, and he praised God.

Daniel told the King the dream and its interpretation. The King stated, "Surely your God is the God of gods and the Lord of kings and revealer of mysteries, for you were able to reveal this mystery" (*v.47*).

This story confirms that God communicates with all His people (the just and the unjust); and **He** has the interpretation.

Daniel and his friends prayed and praised God.

The dream reveals provision and warning.

As I reflect on the character of King Nebuchadnezzar, this scripture comes to mind:

"The earth is the Lord's, and everything in it, the world, and all who live in it." – *Psalm 24:1*

The next biblical person is Joseph. I selected him because:

(1) On the dedication page, I asked Xoana if she was Joseph.

(2) He is the poster child for God communicating to His people through dreams.

He was 17 years old—a young man, a child some would say—when he had his first dream.

He also had the gift to interpret dreams (*Genesis 37:5–11; Gen 40:5–22; Gen 41:1–40; Gen 41:15–16; Gen 42–46*).

In the second dream (*Gen 37:9–11*), Jacob rebuked Joseph but pondered it.

I felt like Jacob should have known God was speaking to Joseph, because God communicated with Jacob through dreams.

Nonetheless, God's plan is…

Three Points of Encouragement I Would Like to Leave with You:

(1) Family Drama

Joseph's brothers wanted to kill him, but they ended up selling him into slavery.

He was his father's favorite child.

He had a dream they couldn't handle, and they clearly misunderstood.

Psalm 27:10 reads: "When my father and my mother forsake me, then the Lord will take me up."

Even in the extreme cases of abandonment, God remains faithful.

(2) Predatory Intent

He landed at Potiphar's home, appeared to be doing well, but temptation and lies raised their heads.

When Potiphar's wife saw that she would not get her way with Joseph, she accused him of attempted rape.

1 Peter 5:8 states, "Be sober, be vigilant; because your adversary the devil, as a roaring lion, walketh about, seeking whom he may devour."

Despite temptation, we can still resist the enemy and stand on God's Word.

Joseph was thrown into jail, but the story continues.

(3) Purpose Comes from God

Joseph interpreted the cupbearer and baker's dreams (*Genesis 40*), which led him to interpret Pharaoh's dream.

Twenty-two years later, Joseph was appointed second in command over Egypt.

The dream Joseph interpreted for Pharaoh—seven years of overflow and seven years of famine—came to pass.

The famine was region-wide, and Joseph's siblings and the rest of the family eventually had to move to Egypt for food.

I don't want to be messy, but the Word stated that they bowed down and honored him.

We are humbled by Joseph's statement to them and the type of God we serve:

"You intended to harm me, but God intended it for good to accomplish what is now being done, the saving of many lives." (*Genesis 50:20*)

Now, we see the manifestation of God's purpose, protection, and provision—not just for Joseph but for the entire family.

What I am learning is some things may be out of our control, but trust God to always work it out in His divine favor.

Romans 8:28 – "And we know that all things work together for good to them that love God, to them who are called according to his purpose."

God provides provision and protection from generation to generation; and our purpose comes from God.

During the New Testament era, God was still communicating with His people through dreams to bring forth the Savior of the world—His Son, our Redeemer, Jesus.

The story states that Mary was with child, and her husband was a righteous man and was going to divorce her quietly.

After Joseph considered this, an angel of the Lord appeared to him in a dream and told him not to be afraid to take Mary as his wife because the conception was by the Holy Spirit.

The baby would be a son, and you will name him **Jesus** (*Matthew 1:18–20*).

The Bible notes a second and third time that God came to Joseph in a dream.

The second is a warning—an angel appeared to Joseph in the dream and told him to take the child and mother and go to Egypt because Herod wanted to kill the child (*Matthew 2:13*).

The third time, an angel of the Lord appeared to Joseph in a dream and told him to take the child and mother and return to Israel (*Matthew 2:19*).

Observe God's movements to fulfill His purpose for our lives.

Fast forward to the 21st century—I invited two friends to share their God-given dream experiences with us. They are Ms. Daliann James and Ms. Kasba Degrate.

Ms. Daliann James is the Founder of *Each One Lift One*, a women's ministry.

Her dream story is as follows:

God speaks to me in many ways. Dreaming is one that has been more frequent lately.

This story of the dream I had in 2023 was a story of a shift that was about to take place in my life. The year prior, I had just lost my dad to cancer.

I had been working as an entrepreneur in the health and fitness field for 7 years at the time. I felt the need to shift and was not sure in what direction, but I knew I wanted to be financially secure and able to spend quality time with my family—to cherish the moments we have, now that I see how quickly you can lose a loved one.

As a single mother, I had so much to think about. Do I continue doing my fitness business or change the structure so I can have more income but also more quality time with my family?

This was one of many questions and thoughts that I spoke to God about and pondered on daily.

In March of 2023, I had a dream of stepping out of my house with my child on my hip. All I could see was money on the trees, money on the ground, and people coming up to me to put money in my child's hand. It was like money was everywhere.

Although it was a short dream, I knew it was significant.

I remember having a counseling session with my Christian counselor and was telling her about the dream. She gave me a different perspective—that my child being on my hip could also represent my business and/or career.

I pondered on that thought, but I put the dream before the Lord. I didn't immediately get the interpretation, but it was revealed as I went on my way.

One thing I knew for sure was that God was saying, *"Trust me, I'm going to bless you. Don't worry about the finances; I will be with you."*

But how could I not worry when I had bills to pay and didn't know the way?

That same year, I took a step in working part-time at my daughter's school to bring in extra income while I figured out what path to take with my business.

In the meantime, I was writing proposals to restructure my business and go the corporate route. Everything got so overwhelming, and I seemed to have less energy and time to spend with my family.

I knew the Lord wanted me to shift, so I knew I couldn't stay where I was before.

December of 2023, I finally surrendered to the Lord and listened to His instructions—to stop trying to figure it out.

January of 2024, I quit my part-time job and began applying to full-time positions. After my surrender, God gave me a strategy—and it worked!

I was worried about my finances with the shift and being obedient to God, but after I surrendered, I put all my trust in Him. And He really had me covered.

I doubled my income from the part-time job by Ubering and still doing some fitness jobs on the side—with time to spare—and I wasn't worried about anything.

March of 2024, I accepted a temporary contract position on post working in my field as a health tech. Three months later, I was promoted to a permanent position as a *Health Educator.*

This is what God was showing me—He had me covered; I just had to trust Him.

Now I still do health, wellness, and fitness events and services upon request as extra income, but God has secured me financially and given me the time I desire with my family outside of work.

I've been promoted again this year with a significant increase that would take some people years to receive.

When I think back on this dream, I believe it is still unfolding and manifesting.

Ms. Kasba Degrate, *Intelligent Minds Proving & Applying Commitment (IMPAC) Outreach,* a youth non-profit organization, sat down with my mom to ask some questions about what my grandmother talked about that day when this happened.

The dream is as follows:

In June of 1989, when I was ten years old, my grandmother had a troubling dream. She later told me she saw a shadow of danger hanging over myself or my sister, as if something terrible was waiting just outside our home.

When she woke up, the uneasiness remained with her. That morning, she moved around the house trying to keep us occupied.

"Stay here," she urged, handing us small chores. "Don't go anywhere today."

Her voice wasn't just firm—it carried a weight I didn't yet understand.

She shared her interpretation with my mom later that morning. "Something bad is going to happen," she warned. "Don't let them go to that pool."

My mom, exhausted from working long hours and wanting us to have a little fun, tried to brush it off. "They'll be fine, Mama," she replied. "They're just going swimming. Nothing's going to happen."

But my grandmother wouldn't let it go. "You don't understand—I can feel it. Keep them here." Her voice rose with urgency, but my sister and I only felt excitement at the thought of leaving the house, convinced she was being overly protective.

That afternoon, her dream unfolded. The pool was crowded, noisy, and overflowing with people.

At first, we stayed in the shallow end, but the crowd pushed me closer to the deep side. I held on to the edge, small and fragile, until a sudden bump from behind knocked me in.

"Help!" I tried to cry, but water filled my mouth and pulled me under. I didn't know how to swim.

The sounds of laughter and splashing faded as everything went silent.

Later, I was told that a young man pulled me out, but I was already unconscious.

Nearly 24 hours later, I woke up in a hospital bed, tubes down my throat, and my hands tied so I wouldn't pull them out.

As I lay there, weak but alive, my grandmother's words echoed in my mind: *"Something bad is going to happen."*

Her dream had not only been a warning, but it had also been a foreshadowing of the moment that nearly took my life.

In summary, God has communicated to Ms. Daliaan through a dream that He is going to release unlimited provision for her and her child.

Philippians 4:19 (KJV): *"But my God shall supply all your need according to His riches in glory by Christ Jesus."*

Ms. Kasba lives today to share her grandmother's dream.

I want to reinforce that just because my child died does not mean your child has to die. God is a healer, and we need to be fully persuaded *(Romans 4:20-21)*—total confidence without wavering—that He will heal us.

Other Ways God Communicates with Us

So, you say, *"Irma, God does not communicate with me through dreams."*

My response is—God is not limited, and as believers, we should be aware of all the ways God communicates with us.

This section was inspired by three sisters in Christ that I surveyed about how God communicates with them. Their response is as such:

Sister Jimmy Lee with Kingdom Life Church stated that "God speaks to her through His word, songs, and moments of reflection."

Ms. Yvonne Osborne's response was that "God rarely speaks to her through dreams, but through visions. The Act of Grace ministry, a youth bible club in Jamaica, was a vision from God birth by His word.

Sister Denise Moore with Kingdom Life Church states that "God communicates with her through the preaching of His word, reading His word, and the Holy Spirit."

Here are some other ways God communicates with us:

The Bible – 2 Timothy 3:16–17

The Holy Spirit – John 14:26

Prayer – Jeremiah 33:3

Prophets & Messengers – Amos 3:7

Circumstances – Romans 8:28

Nature and Creation – Psalm 19:1

Audible Voice – John 12:28

Angels – Matthew 1:20

Through Other Believers – Proverbs 27:17

Whichever way God communicates with you, I hope you perceive it.

Chapter 7

In the End

In My Father's house are many mansions; if it were not so, I would have told you. I go to prepare a place for you, I will come again and receive you to Myself; that where I am, there you may be also.

— John 14: 2 – 3 (NKJV)

Dream Journal

Date: _____

Time you woke up: _____

Title of the Dream: _____

The Dream (Detailed Description):

_____

_____

_____

Emotions Felt (Peaceful, Afraid, Confused, Joyful, Urgent, Other):

_____

_____

Interpretation:

_____

_____

Scripture or Insight:

_____

_____

Manifestation (which may come later):

_____

_____

_____

A God-given dream has its purposes, which is for us to live a life orchestrated by God.

To our children, in the end, parents can only take you so far in life, and you need to know God for yourself. God will never leave you or forsake you (Hebrews 13:5); and Jesus promises that He will be with us even to the end (Matthew 28:20).

Parents, teach your children about God. I am a witness. I have partially shared my childhood and adulthood. God has proven to me that He is with me.

The death of my 9-year-old daughter brought my faith into question.

Irma, do you really believe when you accept Jesus Christ as your Lord and Savior that you have eternal life, and one day we will be reunited with Him and our loved ones who passed on in Christ before us?

Read the promises from Paul in 1 Thessalonians 4:13–18 (NIV):

"Brothers and sisters, we do not want you to be uninformed about those who sleep in death, so that you do not grieve like the rest of mankind, who have no hope. For we believe that Jesus died and rose again, and so we believe that God will bring with Jesus those who have fallen asleep in Him... And so we will be with the Lord forever. Therefore encourage one another with these words."

Our children are experiencing challenges maneuvering through life daily.

I have been given an opportunity by Intelligent Minds Proving & Applying Commitment (IMPAC) Outreach, a non-profit organization founded by Dr. Rodney Duckett, to teach cooking classes to young men in the juvenile system. I am not privy to their cases, but it's not for good behavior.

"The thief (enemy) comes only to steal, kill, and destroy; but Christ comes that we may live and live life more abundantly." — John 10:10

Even the best of us parenting in Christ, the enemy will come in and try to snatch our children.

But God loves us and our children.

The Word of God also lets us know in 2 Peter 3:9, "The Lord is not slack concerning His promise, as some count slackness, but is longsuffering toward us, not willing that any should perish but that all should come to repentance."

I leave you with this universal life-changing recitation that we say and believe at Kingdom Life Church.

It's as easy as **A, B, C** to accept Jesus Christ as our Lord and Savior:

A – Accept that you are a sinner and need God's forgiveness. *(Romans 3:23)*

B – Believe that Jesus is God's Son, who died for your sins and rose again. *(Acts 16:31)*

C – Confess Jesus as your Lord and Savior. *(Romans 10:9)*

Find yourself a good Bible-based church where parents and children can grow in faith and be surrounded by other believers.

In closing, John 3:16 reminds us:

"For God so loved the world, that He gave His only begotten Son, that whosoever believeth in Him should not perish, but have everlasting life."

Not only did He provide salvation for His people, but He also left us the Holy Spirit who lives in us. He has not forsaken us, and one way He communicates His message with us is through dreams.

I hope you perceive it.

Meet the Author

Chef Irma Gottshalk is the chef-owner of *iGott Flava Catering, LLC* and the author of *Bless Up! Respect and Manner: Cook and Eat Jamaican Food Weekly*.

The beloved wife of Kevin and mother to Aletheia and Xoana. Irma is also deeply rooted in her faith as a child of God.

Currently, she is working on her second book, *God-Given Dream: One Evidence God Communicates with His People*, inspired by a divine vision that also led her to begin developing a bed and breakfast in Jamaica.

Her story is one of determination, resilience, and reinvention. After migrating to the United States from Jamaica, Irma completed high school and enlisted in the U.S. Army, serving honorably as an Administrative and HR Specialist for 22 years before retiring.

Retirement marked not an ending, but a new beginning. Pursuing her long-standing passion for food, she attended *Le Cordon Bleu College of Culinary Arts*, immersed herself in global cuisines, and soon after opened her own Jamaican-Caribbean restaurant — a vibrant space where every dish celebrated culture, heritage, and community.

Today, through *iGott Flava Catering*, teaching youth cooking classes with nonprofit organizations, and her writing, Chef Irma continues to weave together her love for food, faith, and culture.

She believes that both cooking and serving others are ministries — expressions of God's creativity and love — and she strives to inspire others to embrace their God-given dreams with courage and faith.